$\mathcal{E}$ASY STOVETOP CHICKEN

CONTENTS

CHICKEN DISHES FROM AROUND THE WORLD

Experience the versatility of chicken as it's prepared across the globe. Whether spicy, tangy, or aromatic; fried, sautéed, or stewed; poultry readily adapts to each culture's cuisine.

LATIN AMERICA & THE CARIBBEAN

In the bustling markets of this part of the world, you'll always hear the clucking of hens, which are prized for their eggs as well as their meat. Cooked in traditional dishes with fiery spices and exotic fruits and vegetables, chicken is the protein of choice in Latin America and the Caribbean islands. Colorful, zesty dishes—like creole-spiced chicken with pineapple and spicy Mexican enchiladas—impart the warm spirit and vibrant personality of these lands.

ASIA & THE FAR EAST

The wok is widely used in Asia—it's the perfect tool for cooking up bite-size pieces of chicken with vegetables or fruit. The quick stir-fry method is easy and yields excellent

NORTH AMERICA & AUSTRALIA

Health-conscious Americans and Australians value tasty chicken meat for its low fat and cholesterol content.

WESTERN EUROPE & THE MEDITERRANEAN

NORTHERN & EASTERN EUROPE

Robust and hearty chicken dishes are always a hit with the people of these rustic northern regions. They love their poultry breaded and fried a crispy, golden brown—and sometimes filled with soft, melted cheese or topped with a rich, simply seasoned cream sauce.

NORTH AFRICA & THE MIDDLE EAST

Fragrant spices and herbs—sold in lively marketplaces—lend North African and Middle Eastern poultry dishes extraordinary flavor and brilliant color. Cooks here often combine sweet and savory ingredients in dishes like braised chicken with dried fruits and honey, or chicken breasts stuffed with fruits, nuts, and rice.

results with the popular recipes of these regions. Garlic, ginger, and soy sauce are among the favorite seasonings for chicken dishes, which are often served atop noodles or rice.

Wild herbs, olive oil, garlic, and fresh tomatoes are classic ingredients of Mediterranean cuisine. Cooks in this part of the world gently simmer poultry in various sauces until it's mouthwateringly tender.

FRUITED CHICKEN CURRY

INDIA

Here's something scrumptious from the land of the Taj Mahal—tender chicken in a sauce of fresh pineapple, delicate mango, toasted coconut flakes, and mild curry.

INGREDIENTS
(Serves 4)

- 1 pound skinless boneless chicken breasts
- ¼ cup all-purpose flour
- salt, white pepper
- 1 mango
- ½ pineapple
- 3 shallots
- 2 tablespoons vegetable oil
- 1 tablespoon minced fresh ginger
- 1 tablespoon mild curry powder
- 1 cup chicken broth
- ¼ cup coconut milk
- 2 tablespoons sweetened shredded coconut

INGREDIENT TIP

In India, the spice mixes for a curry depend on familial and regional formulas. During the 19th century, British colonists introduced a ready-made curry powder to Europe.

1 Rinse the chicken in cold water, pat dry, and cut into ½-inch strips. On a plate, mix the flour with ½ teaspoon salt, and ¼ teaspoon pepper, and use to coat the chicken pieces.

Step 1

2 Peel the mango, pineapple, and shallots. Slice the mango flesh from the pit and remove the pineapple core. Cut all the fruit into bite-size pieces and place in a medium bowl. Finely mince the shallots.

Step 2

3 Heat the oil in a wok or large skillet over medium heat. Shake off the excess flour from the chicken and brown in hot oil for 2 minutes, stirring. Remove from the pan and drain on paper towels.

4 In the oil in the pan, sauté the shallots and ginger for 4 minutes or until browned. Stir in the fruit, curry powder, and broth. Boil for 5 minutes. Add the chicken and coconut milk. Simmer, covered, over low heat for 5 minutes.

Step 4

5 In a small ungreased skillet, toast the coconut over medium heat for 5–8 minutes. Sprinkle it over the curry just before serving.

Preparation: 30 minutes
Cooking: 20 minutes
Per serving: 370 cal; 29 g pro; 13 g fat; 35 g carb.

TYPICALLY INDIAN
Holiday meals in India often include curried chicken. In Kerala, a fertile region in southwestern India, home-raised hens and wild ducks found on local waters are used in poultry dishes by the inhabitants of the area.

COOKING TIP

If you use a large nonstick skillet instead of a wok for frying, you can reduce the amount of oil you use by half, since the pan's coating prevents the ingredients from sticking. It's best to brush the pan lightly with vegetable oil (or wipe it with a paper towel dipped in oil) when you start, to ensure even cooking.

SERVING TIPS

The curry goes well with a sweet-and-sour mango chutney and aromatic basmati rice.

Iced mint tea makes a refreshing accompaniment to this dish.

CRUNCHY CASHEW CHICKEN

THAILAND

Toasted cashews and stir-fried chicken breasts in a flavorful glaze of rice wine and soy sauce make for a simple dish that's wonderfully fragrant.

INGREDIENTS
(Serves 4)

- ¼ cup light soy sauce
- ¼ cup rice wine or sherry
- 1 egg white
- salt, black pepper
- 6 tablespoons oil
- 1 pound skinless boneless chicken breasts
- 4 scallions
- ½ pound mushrooms
- ⅓ cup cashews
- 1 tablespoon minced fresh ginger
- 1 cup chicken broth
- 1 tablespoon cornstarch

INGREDIENT TIPS

• Cashews are rich in minerals and vitamin E and lend a slightly sweet taste to this dish.
• Rice wine can be found in specialty food markets and Asian grocery stores; if you are unable to find it, sherry makes a good substitute.

1 In a medium bowl, mix the soy sauce, rice wine, egg white, ½ teaspoon salt, ¼ teaspoon pepper, and 2 tablespoons oil. Rinse the chicken in cold water, pat dry, and cut into ½-inch cubes. Toss the chicken in the soy-sauce marinade and let stand for 30 minutes. Clean the scallions and cut into thin rings. Rinse the mushrooms in cold water, dry on paper towels, and quarter.

Step 1

2 Heat 2 tablespoons oil in a wok or large skillet over medium heat. Add the cashews and cook, stirring, for 30 seconds, until brown. Transfer to a small bowl. Drain the chicken and reserve the marinade. Gradually add the chicken to the wok, and cook, stirring, for 2–3 minutes, until cooked through. Transfer the chicken to a plate.

Step 2

3 Add the remaining oil to the wok. Fry the scallions and ginger for 2 minutes, until fragrant and soft, stirring constantly. Then add the mushrooms and cook for 4 minutes, until soft.

4 In a small bowl, mix the marinade, broth, and cornstarch, and add to the mixture in the wok. Boil for 1 minute. Stir in the chicken and cashews. Serve immediately.

Step 3

Preparation: 30 minutes
Marinating: 30 minutes
Cooking: 10 minutes
Per serving: 439 cal; 32 g pro;
28 g fat; 13 g carb.

TYPICALLY THAI
One of the favorite cooking techniques in Thailand is stir-frying: Cut-up pieces of meat and vegetables are briefly sautéed with a little oil in a hot wok. With this method, the ingredients' flavor, color, texture, and nutrients are well preserved.

COOKING TIP

You can replace the fresh ginger in this recipe with 1 tablespoon ground ginger, but you'll sacrifice the pungent, spicy aroma that the fresh seasoning has to offer. One of ginger's many uses in natural medicine is as an aid for digestion—another reason to include it in your cooking!

SERVING TIPS

For extra seasoning, offer soy sauce and Asian chili sauce, available in the ethnic food section of most supermarkets.

 Serve with white wine spritzers or hot rice wine in little porcelain bowls.

SERVING TIPS If you like, try eating this dish with chopsticks, and serve with a soy dipping sauce.

Green tea or fruit juice—mango would go nicely—are good beverages for this meal.

CHICKEN-NOODLE STIR-FRY

SINGAPORE

INGREDIENTS
(Serves 4)

- 1 pound skinless boneless chicken breasts
- 5 tablespoons soy sauce
- 1 tablespoon white vinegar
- ½ pound vermicelli
- ¼ cup peanut oil
- 1 can (15 ounces) bamboo shoots, drained
- 1 jalapeño chile
- 3 scallions
- 1 garlic clove
- 1 tablespoon cornstarch
- 1 tablespoon minced fresh ginger
- 1½ cups bean sprouts

INGREDIENT TIP
Instead of vermicelli, use Asian cellophane noodles. These noodles don't need to be precooked; just soften in hot water for 5–10 minutes before adding to the wok.

This tasty one-dish meal features the spiciness of garlic, ginger, and jalapeño. It requires minimal preparation and can be cooked up in your wok in a flash.

1 Rinse the chicken in cold water, pat dry, and cut into ½-inch-thick strips. Mix 3 tablespoons of the soy sauce and the vinegar in a medium bowl. Toss the chicken in soy-sauce marinade; let stand for 30 minutes.

2 In a large saucepan of boiling salted water, cook the vermicelli for 4 minutes. Drain in a colander and rinse with cold water. Drizzle with 1 tablespoon oil and toss to coat. Cut the bamboo shoots into thin strips, and the jalapeño and scallions diagonally into rings. Mince the garlic.

3 Remove the chicken from the marinade. Drain, and then toss the chicken in the cornstarch. Heat the remaining oil in a wok or large skillet. Stir-fry the garlic and ginger for 1 minute. Add the chicken and stir-fry for 2–3 minutes, until cooked through. Push the chicken to one side.

4 Add the bamboo shoots, jalapeño, and scallions; stir-fry for 2–3 minutes. Add the bean sprouts and noodles last and stir-fry for 1–2 minutes. Sprinkle the chicken mixture with the remaining 2 tablespoons soy sauce; toss to distribute evenly. Serve immediately.

Step 1

Step 2

Step 4

Preparation: 30 minutes
Marinating: 30 minutes
Cooking: 10 minutes
Per serving: 505 cal; 37 g pro; 16 g fat; 52 g carb.

TYPICALLY SINGAPOREAN
Ginger is essential to Asian cuisine, including that of Singapore. This aromatic seasoning has thrived for 2,000 years in tropical climates, and has been used to flavor both sweet and savory dishes. Singaporean cooks enjoy the flavor it adds to meats, fish, and shellfish.

$\mathscr{G}$OLDEN CHICKEN TERIYAKI

JAPAN

When company is on the way, whip up this enticing Japanese delicacy in a marinade of sesame, ginger, and honey—your guests will love it.

INGREDIENTS
(Serves 4)

- 1⅓ pounds skinless boneless chicken breasts
- 2 cloves garlic
- 1-inch piece fresh ginger
- 2 tablespoons soy sauce
- 1½ tablespoons tahini
- 1 tablespoon honey
- 3 tablespoons oil
- 2 scallions
- 1 small cucumber

INGREDIENT TIP

A traditional Japanese recipe might grind sesame seeds to use in the chicken coating. For an easier, updated version, tahini (the Middle Eastern pureed sesame-seed paste) is used here.

1 Rinse the chicken in cold water, pat dry, and cut into 1-inch cubes. Peel and coarsely mince the garlic and ginger.

2 Place the garlic, ginger, soy sauce, tahini, honey, and 1 tablespoon oil in a large bowl. Add the chicken and stir to coat. Cover and let stand in the refrigerator for about 2 hours.

3 Clean the scallions and finely chop. Wash the cucumber, cut into thin rounds, and arrange the slices on a large platter.

4 Heat the remaining oil in a large skillet or wok over medium-high heat. Add the chicken and the marinade and stir-fry for 2–4 minutes, until brown on all sides. Add ¼ cup water; simmer, covered, over low heat for 5 minutes, until cooked through.

5 Arrange the chicken over the cucumber slices. Sprinkle with the scallions and serve immediately.

Step 1

Step 2

Step 3

Preparation: 20 minutes
Marinating: 2 hours
Cooking: 12 minutes
Per serving: 321 cal; 37 g pro; 15 g fat; 9 g carb.

TYPICALLY JAPANESE

Japanese cooks know that high-quality ingredients make all the difference, and always choose the freshest and best meats, fruits, and vegetables. They are known for the care they put into the colorful, delicate presentation of a meal.

COOKING TIP

Try adding 3–4 tablespoons of Japanese rice wine or sherry and 1 tablespoon of grated orange peel to the marinade. Then replace the sesame seeds with roasted peanuts. These steps will dramatically change the flavor of this dish.

SERVING TIPS

For a side dish, make a salad of shredded cabbage and carrots. Serve the chicken and salad with white or brown rice.

 Jasmine tea or rice wine make refreshing accompaniments to this meal.

CHICKEN STIR-FRY—THREE WAYS

Choose from a trio of exotic sauces—harmonious combinations of Far Eastern ingredients—to add flavor to simple stir-fried chicken.

BASIC CHICKEN RECIPE

With only a few special ingredients on hand, you can create three delicious dishes from this stir-fry.

(SERVES 4)

- 4 skinless boneless chicken breasts
- 2 garlic cloves
- 4 scallions
- 1 cup bean sprouts
- ¼ cup vegetable oil
- 1 tablespoon minced fresh ginger

1 Rinse the chicken in cold water, dry, and cut into ½-inch cubes.

2 Peel and mince garlic. Wash the scallions and cut into thin rings. Rinse the bean sprouts in cold water and pat dry.

3 Heat the oil in a large skillet or wok. Stir-fry the chicken for 4 minutes over high heat. Push the chicken to the side, then add garlic, scallions and ginger. Cook, stirring, for 2 minutes. Add the sprouts; cook 1 minute.

CHICKEN IN SWEET-AND-SOUR SAUCE

Preparation: 20 minutes   Cooking: 10 minutes

CHINA

FOR THE SAUCE

- 1 medium tomato
- ¼ cup soy sauce
- ¼ cup red wine vinegar
- 1 tablespoon sugar
- ⅛ teaspoon ground black pepper
- 2 ounces roasted peanuts, coarsely chopped

4 Reserve the bean sprouts from the basic recipe. Cube the tomato and add to the chicken-garlic mixture. Cook for 1 minute.

5 In a bowl, mix the soy sauce, vinegar, sugar, and pepper; stir into the chicken. Bring to a boil. Add the sprouts; cook 1 minute. Sprinkle with peanuts.

CHICKEN IN COCONUT SAUCE

Preparation: 15 minutes   Cooking: 10 minutes

INDONESIA

FOR THE SAUCE
- 1 can (8 ounces) coconut milk
- 1-2 tablespoons soy sauce or oyster sauce
- 1 dried chile pepper, crushed, or ¼ teaspoon crushed red pepper

4 Reserve the bean sprouts from the basic recipe. Add the coconut milk to the chicken-garlic mixture, and bring to a boil. Simmer over medium heat for 5 minutes.

5 Stir in the soy sauce and chile. Add the sprouts; cook 1 minute.

CHICKEN IN SPICY GINGER SAUCE

Preparation: 20 minutes   Cooking: 10 minutes

VIETNAM

FOR THE SAUCE
- 1 tomato
- 1-2 dried chile peppers, crushed, or ½ teaspoon crushed red pepper
- 1 tablespoon minced fresh ginger
- 3 tablespoons red wine vinegar
- 2 tablespoons soy sauce
- 1 tablespoon dark sesame oil

4 Reserve the bean sprouts from the basic recipe. Cube the tomato and add to the chicken-garlic mixture. Cook for 1 minute.

5 In a bowl, mix the chiles, ginger, vinegar, soy sauce, and sesame oil; stir into the chicken. Bring to a boil. Add the sprouts; cook 1 minute.

HONEY-MUSTARD CHICKEN SALAD

Here's a delicious, unusual combination—tender cubes of chicken and sweet melon balls in a zippy mixture of mustard and honey. The dish makes a refreshing lunch or light dinner.

INGREDIENTS
(Serves 4)

- 1 pound skinless boneless chicken breasts
- 2 garlic cloves
- 3 tablespoons vegetable oil
- salt, black pepper
- 1 tablespoon honey
- 1 tablespoon Dijon mustard
- 1 tablespoon lemon juice or white wine vinegar
- ½ honeydew melon
- 2 kiwis
- a few radicchio leaves
- 1 package radish or alfalfa sprouts (optional)

INGREDIENT TIP

Melons have a very high water content, which makes them great thirst quenchers in hot weather. Try watermelon in place of honeydew for a beautiful touch of color and a crunchy texture.

1 Rinse the chicken in cold water, pat dry with paper towels, and cut into ½-inch cubes. Peel and mince the garlic. Heat 1 tablespoon oil in a large skillet over medium heat. Add the garlic and sauté for 1 minute, until the garlic is fragrant, stirring constantly. Add the chicken, ½ teaspoon salt, and ¼ teaspoon pepper, and cook for 4–5 minutes until lightly browned, stirring constantly. Transfer to a large bowl and cool.

Step 1

2 For the dressing, in a medium bowl, stir together the honey, mustard, and lemon juice. Whisk in 2 tablespoons oil, ½ teaspoon salt, and ¼ teaspoon pepper.

Step 2

3 Remove the seeds from the honeydew melon with a spoon. Scoop out the flesh with a melon baller. Peel the kiwis, cut them in half lengthwise, and then cut into slices.

4 Mix the chicken with the melon balls, kiwi slices, and dressing. Arrange some radicchio on plates and spoon the salad on top. Sprinkle the sprouts over each salad.

Step 3

Preparation: 35 minutes
Cooking: 7 minutes
Per serving: 293 cal; 27 g pro; 14 g fat; 19 g carb.

TYPICALLY AUSTRALIAN
In Australia, which has a temperate climate year-round, people enjoy entertaining outdoors. Fresh salads like this one make perfect seaside fare on a hot day.

COOKING TIP

Prepare this salad in the evening so you can enjoy it as a lunchtime treat at work the next day. To make a richer, creamier version of the dressing, simply mix in 1–2 tablespoons of sour cream or spoon dollops on each portion.

SERVING TIPS

Offer vanilla ice cream with toasted almonds and chocolate sauce for dessert.

A glass of chilled Australian Sauvignon Blanc makes an ideal complement to this meal.

$\mathscr{C}$OLORFUL CHICKEN 'N RICE

USA

This hearty dish from Louisiana combines rice and chicken with tomatoes and both hot and sweet peppers. The warm flavors will remind you of the heat of the South.

INGREDIENTS
(Serves 4–6)

- 3-pound chicken
- 1 *each* red, yellow, and green bell pepper
- 2 jalapeño chiles
- 1 pound tomatoes
- 1 onion
- 2 tablespoons vegetable oil
- ¼ teaspoon cayenne pepper
- salt, black pepper
- 2 cups long-grain white rice
- 1 tablespoon paprika
- 4 cups chicken broth
- ½ cup green olives
- Tabasco sauce

INGREDIENT TIP

When you are choosing chili peppers, keep in mind that color indicates ripeness, not hotness. Red peppers can be sweet rather than fiery. The degree of heat depends on the variety of pepper.

1 Rinse the chicken in cold water, pat dry, and cut into 8–10 pieces. Remove the seeds and veins from the bell peppers and jalapeños. Cut the bell peppers into large chunks; mince the jalapeños. (Rinse hands after handling jalapeños.) In a large saucepan of boiling water, blanch the tomatoes for 30 seconds. Peel and cut into ½-inch dice. Peel and finely chop the onion.

Step 2

2 Heat the oil over medium-high heat in a large skillet. Sprinkle chicken with the cayenne, ½ teaspoon salt, and ¼ teaspoon black pepper. Fry until golden brown, about 5 minutes per side; transfer to a plate. Remove all but 2 tablespoons fat. Sauté the bell peppers for 4 minutes; transfer to a bowl. Sauté the onions until translucent. Add the jalapeños, tomatoes, rice, paprika, and 1½ teaspoons salt. Cook, stirring, for 2 minutes.

Step 2

3 Add the broth, and cook the rice mixture for 10 minutes over low heat. Add the bell peppers and chicken, cover, and simmer for 20 minutes, until the rice is tender.

4 Use a small knife to pit the olives, if needed, then coarsely chop. Stir them into the rice mixture. Add Tabasco to taste.

Step 4

Preparation: 40 minutes
Cooking: 50 minutes
Per serving: 742 cal; 42 g pro;
31 g fat; 71 g carb.

TYPICALLY LOUISIANA

Early Spanish settlers brought their traditional chicken-and-rice dishes to their new Louisiana home. This dish is a close relative of the Spanish *arroz con pollo*. Other famous Louisiana chicken-and-rice combinations include a version of jambalaya using chicken.

COOKING TIP
It's easy to make a quart of your own chicken broth:
In a pot, bring to a boil 2 pounds chicken backs,
wings, and necks; some chopped onion, carrot, and
celery; 10 peppercorns, 6 parsley sprigs, and a bay
leaf; and enough water to cover. Skim off foam and
simmer for 2 hours. Strain the broth and refrigerate.

SERVING TIPS
Sprinkle finely shredded basil or
tarragon over this dish before serving.
Serve extra olives for nibbling.

Add a flavorful accent—a slice of lemon or a sprig
of fresh mint—to your sparkling water or iced tea.

TASTY CHICKEN BURGERS

USA

This updated version of the classic hamburger—made with chicken instead of beef and served with a creamy sauce—is perfect for casual meals with family or friends.

INGREDIENTS
(Serves 4)

- 1 egg
- 1 pound ground chicken or turkey
- salt
- ½ teaspoon paprika
- 1 dill pickle
- 1 tablespoon capers
- ½ cup mayonnaise
- 1-2 teaspoons anchovy paste (optional)
- 3 small tomatoes
- 4 lettuce leaves
- 1 tablespoon vegetable oil
- 4 hamburger buns, split

INGREDIENT TIPS

• Anchovy paste can be found in small tubes at most supermarkets; after opening, keep it in the refrigerator.
• For a more nutritious alternative, buy whole-wheat hamburger buns.

1 Bring 4 cups of water to a boil in a small saucepan, add the egg, and cook over very low heat (do not boil) for 12 minutes. Rinse with cold water until cool.

2 While the egg is cooling, place the chicken in a bowl and add ½ teaspoon salt and the paprika. Shape the mixture into 4 patties.

Step 2

3 Peel and finely chop the egg and place it in a medium bowl. Chop the pickle and capers and add to the egg. Add the mayonnaise and anchovy paste. Wash, dry, and stem the tomatoes, and cut into slices. Wash the lettuce leaves and dry well.

Step 3

4 Heat the oil in a large nonstick skillet over medium-high heat, and fry the burgers for 5 minutes on each side. Cook, covered, 2–3 minutes longer, until no longer pink in the center.

5 While the burgers cook, place a lettuce leaf, several tomato slices, and some sauce on the bottom half of each bun. Add a burger and the top half of a bun.

Step 5

Preparation: 30 minutes
Cooking: 15 minutes
Per serving: 517 cal; 33 g pro; 30 g fat; 27 g carb.

TYPICALLY AMERICAN
An all-beef burger served with fries and a cola has been a fast-food standby since the 1950s, but health-conscious Americans like to substitute ground chicken or turkey for beef in burgers, as well as in tacos and frankfurters.

COOKING TIP

Vary the sauce: Mix together 1 tablespoon ketchup,
2 tablespoons mayonnaise, 1 teaspoon spicy mustard,
a pinch of sugar, 2–3 drops of Tabasco sauce, and salt
and pepper to taste. Or mash together an avocado
half, 1 tablespoon lemon or lime juice, 2 tablespoons
sour cream, and a pinch of salt and pepper.

SERVING TIPS

Top your burger with different
fresh sliced vegetables, such as green
pepper, cucumber, or radicchio.

Choose your favorite ice-cold soft drink to wash
down this terrific home-cooked meal.

21

SERVING TIPS Coconut rice is ideal: Cook the rice in equal parts coconut milk and water.

A refreshing piña colada or rum punch will hit the spot with this dish.

CREOLE CHICKEN CON PIÑA

TRINIDAD

INGREDIENTS
(Serves 4)

- 2½-pound chicken
- salt, black pepper
- 2 tablespoons fresh lemon juice
- 4 celery ribs
- 3 scallions
- 2 jalapeño chiles
- ½ pineapple
- 1 ripe banana
- 2½ tablespoons butter
- ½ cup chicken broth
- ½ teaspoon Tabasco sauce
- a few sprigs of fresh cilantro

INGREDIENT TIP

Before preparation, thaw frozen chicken with safety in mind: Place the frozen, unwrapped chicken in a bowl, cover, and allow it to thaw in the refrigerator for 24 hours. Be sure to wash it well and pat dry with paper towels before cooking.

A perfect mixture of sweet, spicy, and sour ingredients turns this Creole chicken-and-pineapple dish into a pleasure you won't soon forget.

1 Rinse the chicken in cold water, pat dry, and cut into 8–10 pieces. Sprinkle with ½ teaspoon salt, ¼ teaspoon pepper, and the lemon juice.

2 Reserve some celery leaves. Slice the celery, scallions, and jalapeños diagonally. Cut off the pineapple skin. Standing the pineapple on end, cut it lengthwise into fourths and remove the core. Cut the quarters lengthwise into slices. In a small bowl, with a fork, mash the banana well.

3 Melt the butter in a large skillet over medium heat. Fry the chicken until browned, about 5 minutes on each side, and transfer to a platter. Add the celery, scallions, jalapeños, and pineapple, and fry for 5 minutes. Remove all but 2 tablespoons of fat from the pan. Stir in the banana and chicken broth, then add the chicken and Tabasco. Cook, covered, for 20 minutes.

4 While the chicken cooks, wash and pat dry the cilantro and remove the leaves. Reserve a few leaves and finely chop the remainder. When the chicken is done, stir in the chopped cilantro. Sprinkle with the celery and cilantro leaves.

Step 3

Step 3

Step 4

Preparation: 35 minutes
Cooking: 30 minutes
Per serving: 557 cal; 36 g pro; 35 g fat; 27 g carb.

TYPICALLY TRINIDAD
Tropical fruits like pineapple and banana are wonderful complements to hearty Trinidadian meals. The pineapple found its way to the Caribbean from South America, and the banana crossed over to the New World from Asia as early as the 16th century.

COCONUT-FRIED CHICKEN

Caribbean cuisine is rich with the flavors of rum, coconut, and tropical fruits. This vibrant chicken dish will virtually transport you to the island paradise of Jamaica.

INGREDIENTS
(Serves 4–6)

- 2 garlic cloves
- salt
- 3 limes
- 2 tablespoons mango nectar or peach nectar
- ⅓ cup dark rum (optional)
- 3-pound chicken
- ½ cup + ⅓ cup all-purpose flour
- ½ teaspoon white pepper
- 1 cup unsweetened shredded coconut
- 2 eggs
- 1 cup peanut oil
- 1 mango

INGREDIENT TIPS

- You can find unsweetened coconut in health-food or specialty stores.
- Finely chopped pecans or walnuts make a good alternative to coconut breading.

1 To make the marinade, peel the garlic, sprinkle with ⅛ teaspoon salt, and mash with a fork. Place in a large bowl. Stir in the juice of 1 lime, the mango nectar, and rum.

Step 1

2 Rinse the chicken in cold water, pat dry, and cut into 8–10 pieces. Place in the marinade and turn to coat. Cover and refrigerate for about 1 hour, turning the pieces occasionally.

3 In a shallow bowl, mix ½ cup flour with 1 teaspoon salt and the white pepper. In another shallow bowl, mix the coconut with ⅓ cup flour. In a third shallow bowl, beat the eggs with 2 tablespoons oil.

Step 3

4 Heat the remaining oil in a large skillet. Remove the chicken from the marinade, roll in the seasoned flour, then in the egg mixture, and finally dredge in the coconut mixture. Fry the chicken pieces for 8 minutes, until golden and cooked through. Drain on paper towels on a baking sheet, and keep warm in a 200°F oven.

Step 4

5 Slice the remaining limes. Peel the mango and cut it into thin slices. Garnish the chicken with the fruit; serve immediately.

Preparation: 20 minutes
Marinating: 1 hour
Cooking: 8 minutes
Per serving: 601 cal; 38 g pro; 48 g fat; 20 g carb.

TYPICALLY JAMAICAN
In the Caribbean, a zest for life and a passion for food go hand in hand—and Jamaica is no exception. Famous for "jerk," their spicy dry rub, Jamaican cooks also make creative use of the foods and beverages native to their island, such as the coconut and rum used above.

COOKING TIPS

• If the mango is very soft and juicy, be sure to
peel and cut it when you start the recipe so that
you can collect its juice and use it for the marinade.
• Don't let the oil become so hot during frying that it
begins to smoke, because the coconut breading will
brown too quickly and burn.

SERVING TIPS

Serve this dish with a little salad
of carrots, zucchini, avocado,
tomato, and lettuce.

Ice-cold water or seltzer with a squirt of lemon
or lime juice makes a refreshing accompaniment.

SPICY CHICKEN MEXICANA

MEXICO

This piquant meal, with its fuss-free preparation and lively ingredients—particularly the hot chiles—is certain to make you an admirer of Mexican food.

INGREDIENTS

(Serves 4)

- 4 skinless boneless chicken breast halves, (1½ pounds total)
- 1 large tomato
- 1 white onion
- 2 garlic cloves
- ⅓ cup walnuts
- 1 *each* green and red bell pepper
- 2 jalapeño chiles
- 2 tablespoons vegetable oil
- salt, cayenne pepper
- ½ cup chicken broth
- 2 tablespoons white-wine vinegar
- 3 dashes Tabasco sauce
- 4 ounces aged Gouda or Monterey Jack cheese

INGREDIENT TIP

Bell peppers can be refrigerated for up to 2 weeks in a perforated plastic bag.

1 Rinse the chicken in cold water and pat dry. In a large saucepan of boiling water, blanch the tomato for 30 seconds, then peel and quarter. Peel the onion and garlic; quarter the onion. Puree the tomato, onion, garlic, and walnuts in a food processor.

2 Cut the bell peppers and jalapeños in half. Remove the seeds and veins and wash. Cut the bell peppers into 1-inch pieces and finely chop the jalapeños. Heat the oil in a large skillet over medium-high heat. Fry the chicken until well browned, 2–4 minutes on each side, and transfer to a plate. Sprinkle with ½ teaspoon salt and ⅛ teaspoon cayenne pepper.

3 In the oil remaining in the skillet, sauté all the peppers over medium-high heat for 3 minutes. Add the tomato mixture and cook for 5 minutes. Add the broth, vinegar, Tabasco, ½ teaspoon salt, and ¼ teaspoon cayenne pepper. Place the chicken breasts on top. Cook, covered, for 15–20 minutes.

4 Coarsely grate the cheese and sprinkle it over the chicken. Remove from the heat, cover, and let stand for about 5 minutes, until the cheese melts. Serve immediately.

Step 1

Step 2

Step 4

Preparation: 30 minutes
Cooking: 30 minutes
Per serving: 461 cal; 50 g pro; 23 g fat;13 g carb.

TYPICALLY MEXICAN

Mexicans love chicken and have created fantastic dishes with it using their unique blends of spices and sauces. The Spanish introduced chicken to Mexico, and in exchange, brought turkey—a favorite food of the Aztecs—back with them to Europe.

COOKING TIPS

• If you prefer a less creamy sauce, add the chunks of tomato, onion, garlic, and walnut directly into the pan in Step 3 instead of processing them in Step 1.

• Be sure to wash your hands with warm, soapy water immediately after cutting the spicy chiles to remove the chili oil.

SERVING TIPS

Put out a bottle of Tabasco for those who like to turn up the heat, and serve with crunchy raw vegetables on the side.

A Mexican beer, served with a garnish of lime, will help cool things down.

CHICKEN AND BEAN ENCHILADAS

MEXICO

The ingredients for these tortillas filled with tender chicken can be prepared ahead of time. Then the dish can be ready in a flash later—perfect for hot summer nights!

INGREDIENTS
(Serves 4)

- 1½ pounds skinless boneless chicken breasts
- salt, black pepper
- ½ teaspoon ground cumin
- 1 red onion
- 1 can (10 ounces) kidney beans
- 1 jar (8 ounces) salsa
- ½ head iceberg lettuce
- 8 corn tortillas
- 2 tablespoons vegetable oil
- ½ cup chopped cilantro or parsley
- 6 ounces goat cheese or feta cheese

INGREDIENT TIP

Cumin, with its rich and earthy aroma, is an essential spice in Mexican and Central American cooking. There really is no substitute for it.

1 Rinse the chicken in cold water and pat dry. Cut the chicken breasts into thin strips and sprinkle with 1 teaspoon salt, ½ teaspoon pepper, and the cumin. Peel and finely chop the onion.

2 Pour the beans into a sieve, rinse with cold water, and place in a small saucepan. Add the salsa and heat through over low heat. Keep warm. Rinse the lettuce in cold water, pat dry, and cut into shreds.

3 In a large nonstick skillet, heat the tortillas about 15 seconds per side, wrap in a kitchen towel, and keep warm. Heat the oil in the skillet over medium-high heat, and sauté the chicken for 4–5 minutes, stirring, until golden brown.

4 Place the tortillas on a cutting board and spread with some bean mixture. Top with chicken strips, and lettuce. Roll up the tortillas and place them on a heated platter. Sprinkle the tortillas with the cilantro and onions. Crumble the cheese and sprinkle over the tortillas. Serve immediately.

Step 1

Step 2

Step 4

Preparation: 30 minutes
Cooking: 15 minutes
Per serving: 611 cal; 57 g pro; 24 g fat; 43 g carb.

TYPICALLY MEXICAN

Hardly any meal in Mexico is complete without tortillas—thin corn or wheat pancakes. Enchiladas are tortillas rolled up and filled with hearty ingredients, such as chicken, beef, vegetables, or cheese. Corn tortillas are also made into tacos and tortilla chips.

COOKING TIP

Make your own tortillas, using ½ cup fine corn meal, ½ cup all-purpose flour, 5 tablespoons oil, 1 teaspoon salt, and about ½ cup water. In a medium bowl, knead these ingredients together and set the dough aside, covered, for an hour. Divide the dough into 8 balls, then roll out each to make a thin pancake. Fry the tortillas one by one in a dry skillet for 30–60 seconds.

SERVING TIPS

Make a guacamole appetizer: Mash avocado, salt, lime juice, and minced onion, tomato, garlic, and jalapeños.

Entice appetites with Bloody Marys or spicy tomato juice, garnished with celery ribs.

SERVING TIPS As a side dish, serve warm pita bread or couscous (tiny grains of Moroccan pasta).

A mixture of seltzer water and your favorite fruit juice will taste delicious with this meal.

SPICED CHICKEN TAGINE

MOROCCO

Golden saffron, plump prunes, spicy ginger, and fresh cilantro give this classic dish from North Africa an extraordinary aroma and flavor.

INGREDIENTS
(Serves 4)

- 3-pound chicken
- 3 onions
- ½ cup pitted prunes
- 1 teaspoon paprika
- salt, black pepper
- ½ teaspoon ground ginger
- ¼ teaspoon ground cinnamon
- pinch of saffron threads
- 1 package (10 ounces) frozen lima or fava beans
- fresh cilantro

INGREDIENT TIPS

- To keep cilantro fresh for several days, wash and dry it gently, layer on paper towels, and store in a plastic bag in the refrigerator.
- There's no real substitute for the fine flavor of saffron, although you can approximate the beautiful yellow color with turmeric.

1 Rinse the chicken in cold water, pat dry, and cut into 8–10 pieces. Remove the skin. Place the chicken in a large saucepan.

2 Peel the onions. Cut 1 into thin rings, and add to the chicken pieces. Finely chop 2 onions and set them aside. Add 2 cups water or just enough so that the chicken pieces are barely covered.

Step 2

3 Bring the water to a boil over medium-high heat, reduce the heat to low, and simmer the chicken, covered, for 15 minutes.

4 Add the chopped onions, prunes, paprika, 1 teaspoon salt, ½ teaspoon pepper, the ginger, cinnamon, and saffron to the chicken. Cook, partially covered, for 5 minutes. Add the lima beans, partially cover, and cook 10–15 minutes longer.

Step 4

5 Place the chicken on a warm platter or in a covered earthenware casserole. Wash the cilantro, coarsely chop, and sprinkle it over the chicken before serving.

Step 5

Preparation: 25 minutes
Cooking: 35 minutes
Per serving: 370 cal; 42 g pro; 6 g fat; 38 g carb.

TYPICALLY ARABIC
Many Arabs once led nomadic lives, roaming across inhospitable stretches of desert. Since fresh produce was unavailable, meat from their livestock herds, complemented with dried fruit and spices, was typically the center of each meal.

HONEY-CITRUS CHICKEN

MOROCCO

This sweet and tangy Moroccan specialty beguiles the senses with fresh citrus fruit and a variety of spices. Enjoy a taste of the Middle East with this succulent meal.

INGREDIENTS
(Serves 4-6)

- 3-pound chicken
- ¼ cup honey
- 2 oranges
- 1 lemon
- 1 onion
- 2 garlic cloves
- 2 tablespoons olive oil
- 1 cup chicken broth
- pinch of saffron threads or ½ teaspoon ground turmeric
- ½ teaspoon ground ginger
- salt, black pepper
- ½ cup black olives

INGREDIENT TIP

To obtain saffron, the stigmas of a particular crocus flower are handpicked, then dried, which is why saffron is so expensive. Store this sensitive spice out of direct light.

1 Rinse the chicken in cold water, pat dry, and cut into 8 pieces. Place in a large bowl. Measure the honey and squeeze in the juice from 1 orange and the lemon. Mix well in the measuring cup.

2 Add the honey mixture to the chicken, and toss to coat. Cover and refrigerate for 1 hour, turning the chicken occasionally.

3 Peel the onion and garlic and finely chop. Remove the chicken from the marinade and lightly pat the chicken dry with paper towels; reserve the marinade. Heat the oil in a large skillet over medium-high heat. Sauté the onion and garlic until the onion is translucent, 2–3 minutes. Add the chicken and brown it on both sides, about 6–7 minutes per side.

4 Add the broth and 2 tablespoons of the marinade. Stir in the saffron, ginger, 1 teaspoon salt, and ½ teaspoon pepper. Simmer over low heat for 40 minutes.

5 Peel the second orange and remove the pith. Remove the sections from the membranes. Decorate the chicken with the orange sections and olives.

Step 1

Step 2

Step 5

Preparation: 30 minutes
Marinating: 1 hour
Cooking: 50 minutes
Per serving: 542 cal; 36 g pro; 35 g fat; 20 g carb.

TYPICALLY MOROCCAN
Olive oil, garlic, and lemon juice give the cuisines of North Africa their basic flavor, but spices are the soul of this area's cooking. Merchants in bazaars offer them in breathtaking variety: saffron, cinnamon, anise, coriander, and cardamom are just a few.

COOKING TIP

To section an orange, first cut off the peel with a
small sharp or serrated knife, then cut between the
membranes to release the segments of fruit.

SERVING TIPS

Accompany this dish with raisin rice: Fry
raisins and uncooked rice in olive oil, cover
with broth, and cook over low heat.

 Hot mint tea, sweetened with honey or
sugar, rounds this dish out perfectly.

FRUIT AND RICE-STUFFED CHICKEN BREASTS

LEBANON

INGREDIENTS
(Serves 4)

- ½ cup pitted prunes
- ½ cup raw long-grain rice
- 5 tablespoons oil
- 2 tablespoons honey
- 2 tablespoons lemon juice
- 1 teaspoon curry powder
- 4 skinless boneless chicken breast halves (about 1½ pounds total)
- ¼ cup pine nuts
- ¼ cup raisins
- salt, black pepper
- 1 pinch *each* of allspice, cinnamon, and cloves
- ¼ cup all-purpose flour

INGREDIENT TIP

Allspice, also known as Jamaican pepper, has a strong aroma reminiscent of nutmeg, cinnamon, cloves, and pepper when the small, dried berries are ground.

Transport yourself to the Middle East with this exotic dish: chicken marinated in honey and lemon, with a richly seasoned filling of rice and dried fruits.

1 In a small bowl, cover the prunes with hot water and soak for 1 hour. In a 1-quart saucepan, cook the rice in 1½ cups salted water for 25 minutes. Drain and cool.

2 While the rice cooks, in a cup, mix 1 tablespoon oil, the honey, lemon juice, and curry. Rinse the chicken in cold water; pat dry. With a sharp knife, cut each breast in half horizontally almost all the way through. Place on a plate, brush the outside with the honey mixture. Cover; refrigerate.

3 Toast the pine nuts in a saucepan over medium-high heat. Chop the raisins and prunes; place in a large bowl. Add the rice, pine nuts, ¼ teaspoon pepper, and spices.

4 Open the chicken breasts and place ½ cup rice mixture on each. Fold the chicken over the filling; seal with toothpicks.

5 On a plate, mix the flour, ¼ teaspoon salt, and a pinch of pepper. Coat the chicken with the flour mixture. Heat the remaining oil over medium-high heat in a large skillet. Sauté the chicken on each side for 4 minutes, until golden brown.

Step 3

Step 4

Step 4

Preparation: 10 minutes
Cooking: 25 minutes
Per serving: 608 cal; 45 g pro; 24 g fat; 55 g carb.

TYPICALLY LEBANESE
People are always thirsty during the hot, dry Lebanese summers, and they keep the street vendors in business by buying up their refreshing, ice-cold lemon drinks. The lemon has been very popular in the Middle East since its introduction to the Mediterranean around A.D. 900.

COOKING TIPS

• To save preparation time, and also to use up leftovers, use 1 cup day-old rice for the rice filling.

• Add color and tang to this recipe by substituting dried apricots for the prunes.

SERVING TIPS

Baklava, a honey-nut pastry, is a favorite dessert in Lebanon and makes a wonderful follow-up to the main course.

 Finish with cinnamon tea: Boil 2 cups of water with cinnamon sticks and sweeten to taste.

35

CHICKEN KIEV

UKRAINE

INGREDIENTS
(Serves 4)

- 4 skinless boneless chicken breast halves, (about 1½ pounds total)
- 4 garlic cloves
- 1 lemon
- several sprigs of fresh dill
- salt, black pepper
- 8 tablespoons butter, softened
- ¼ cup all-purpose flour
- 1 egg, lightly beaten
- ¼–½ cup bread crumbs
- ¼ cup vegetable oil

INGREDIENT TIP

A delicious alternative to garlic butter is butter that is mixed with capers and a generous pinch of chopped fresh herbs, such as chives, parsley, or tarragon.

This Ukrainian specialty is a classic dish in restaurants around the world. It features crispy breaded boneless chicken breasts with a rich, garlicky dill butter tucked inside.

1 Rinse the chicken in cold water and pat dry. With a sharp knife, remove the small fillet from each chicken breast. Reserve for another use. Then cut a pocket into one side of each chicken breast.

2 Peel the garlic, and press it into a small bowl using a garlic press. Finely grate the peel from the lemon. Wash the dill, pat dry, and pull off all the leaves. Mix the lemon peel, dill, ¼ teaspoon salt, ⅛ teaspoon pepper, and the butter into the garlic.

Step 2

3 Divide the garlic butter into 4 portions and insert 1 portion into each chicken pocket. Close each opening with a toothpick. Refrigerate for 1 hour so that the butter becomes firm again.

Step 3

4 Place the flour, egg, and bread crumbs in 3 separate shallow bowls. Sprinkle the chicken with ¼ teaspoon salt and ⅛ teaspoon pepper. Dip them into the flour, then the egg, and lastly the bread crumbs.

5 Heat the oil in a medium skillet and fry the chicken breasts over medium-high heat on each side for 4 minutes, until crispy. Serve immediately.

Step 4

Preparation: 45 minutes
Chilling: 1 hour
Cooking: 10 minutes
Per serving: 544 cal; 43 g pro; 34 g fat; 15 g carb.

TYPICALLY UKRAINIAN

It's no wonder that the Ukrainians influenced Russian cuisine so strongly: One of the oldest cities in Europe and a commercial center as early as the 5th century, the Ukrainian metropolis of Kiev became the capital of Kievan Russia in the 9th century.

COOKING TIPS

• Fry the meat in sufficient oil so that the heat penetrates evenly.

• Turkey also works beautifully in this recipe. Cut about 1½ pounds turkey breast into 4 equal pieces, then cut the pockets as described in Step 1.

SERVING TIPS

Typical side dishes are potatoes, brussels sprouts, cabbage, or peas. A colorful mixed salad also goes well with this meal.

 For an authentic touch, serve your guests hot tea. Well-chilled vodka also goes well.

CREAMY CHICKEN PAPRIKASH

HUNGARY

INGREDIENTS
(Serves 4)

- 2½-pound chicken
- 1 onion
- 1 garlic clove
- 2 red bell peppers
- 2 tablespoons vegetable oil
- ½ cup chicken broth
- ¼ cup white wine
- salt, white pepper
- ¾ cup sour cream
- ¼ cup low-fat yogurt
- 1 tablespoon paprika

INGREDIENT TIP

Try buying free-range chickens, which are raised without hormones and given more room to roam than mass-produced birds. Some say the meat possesses a richer, more "chickeny" flavor.

The venerable Hungarian city of Budapest beckons you with this traditional dish. It's made of bright red peppers and golden brown chicken in a flavorful creamy sauce.

1 Rinse the chicken with cold water, pat dry, and cut into 8 pieces with poultry scissors. Peel and finely chop the onion and garlic. Cut the red peppers into fourths, remove seeds and veins, and rinse. Cut the fourths into large chunks.

Step 1

2 Heat the oil in a large skillet over medium-high heat. Brown the chicken on all sides and remove to a plate. Add the onion to the pan and cook for 1 minute, until transparent. Add the garlic and red peppers and cook for 5 minutes. Return the chicken to the pan.

Step 2

3 Pour in the broth and white wine and add ½ teaspoon salt and ¼ teaspoon pepper. Cover and simmer the chicken over low heat for about 30 minutes. Remove the chicken to a plate. In a bowl, mix the sour cream with the yogurt and paprika. Whisk into the braising sauce.

Step 3

4 Return the chicken to the pan. Remove the pan from the heat and allow the dish to steep, covered, for 5 minutes. Serve in the pan or in a heated bowl.

Preparation: 20 minutes
Cooking: 45 minutes
Per serving: 491 cal; 31 g pro; 37 g fat; 8 g carb.

TYPICALLY HUNGARIAN
Fresh sweet peppers and paprika are to Hungary what beer is to Bavaria. In early summer, Hungarian markets are ablaze with fiery red and deep green peppers. Hungarian paprika, which is made by grinding dried sweet red pepper pods, is of the finest quality.

COOKING TIP

Red peppers are most affordable from summer to late fall, so set some aside for winter by blanching them quickly in boiling water, letting them cool, and freezing them in airtight bags. Frozen peppers can be used in dishes that call for stewing or braising, in which their flavor, not their texture, is important.

SERVING TIPS

Steamed green beans and boiled potatoes go particularly well with chicken paprikash.

Enjoy a glass of fruity white Hungarian Tokay with this savory chicken dish.

SERVING TIPS The perfect dessert to follow this
dish is apple strudel with vanilla ice cream.

Enjoy a glass of dry white wine, cold apple cider,
or sparkling water with this meal.

CRISPY-COATED CHICKEN

AUSTRIA

INGREDIENTS
(Serves 4)

- 2 small chickens or Cornish game hens (about 1½ pounds each)
- ½ cup all-purpose flour
- 1 cup bread crumbs
- salt, black pepper
- 2 eggs
- 3 tablespoons milk
- 1¼ cups vegetable oil
- 1 whole lemon
- 12 sprigs curly parsley, stems removed

INGREDIENT TIP

For a particularly fine breading, substitute crackers for the bread crumbs. Crush ¼ cup crackers in a plastic bag. If you choose this method, use salt-free crackers or cut down the amount of salt used in the breading (Step 1).

For generations, Austrians have savored this simple dish, which features small chicken pieces that are lightly breaded and fried to a crispy brown. Juicy lemon wedges add a tangy flair.

1 Rinse the birds in cold water, pat dry, and cut each into 4 pieces. Place the flour, bread crumbs, and eggs into separate shallow bowls. Stir ¾ teaspoon salt and ½ teaspoon pepper into the flour. Whisk the eggs with the milk.

2 Dip the chicken pieces into the flour and shake off any excess. Then dip the pieces into the egg mixture. Finally dredge them in the bread crumbs. Lightly press the breading onto the hens.

Step 2

3 Heat the oil in 2 large skillets over medium-high heat. Fry the chicken pieces for 20 minutes, turning often and adjusting the heat as necessary. Drain on paper towels and place on a preheated platter.

Step 3

4 While the chickens cook, cut the lemon lengthwise into eighths. Wash the parsley, dry it, and fry it in the oil after the chicken is done. Garnish the chicken pieces with the lemon wedges and parsley, and serve immediately.

Step 4

Preparation: 30 minutes
Cooking: 20 minutes
Per serving: 706 cal; 41 g pro; 44 g fat; 35 g carb.

TYPICALLY VIENNESE

Austrian gourmets can find everything they need at the famous Nasch market. The word "nosh," which Americans sometimes use to mean snack, originated from the German word *naschen,* meaning "to eat on the sly."

CHICKEN GRUYÈRE

SWITZERLAND

INGREDIENTS
(Serves 4)

- 8 chicken breast cutlets (1½ pounds total)
- 4 thick slices Gruyère cheese (4 ounces total)
- ⅔ cup bread crumbs
- 2 tablespoons all-purpose flour
- 1 egg
- salt, white pepper
- ½ cup vegetable oil

IN ADDITION

- Italian parsley
- 1 lemon

INGREDIENT TIP

Gruyère is a Swiss cheese made from cow's milk. Similar to Emmentaler, though significantly sharper, it's easy to grate and ideal for sauces, fondues, and stuffings.

This popular Swiss dish is surprisingly easy to prepare. It features a smooth layer of melted Gruyère cheese nestled between two tender pieces of chicken breast.

1 Rinse the chicken breasts in cold water and pat dry. On each of 4 pieces, lay a slice of cheese and top with another piece of chicken. Secure with toothpicks. Place on a plate and cover.

Step 1

2 Place the bread crumbs, flour, and egg in separate bowls. Stir 1 teaspoon salt and ¼ teaspoon white pepper into the bread crumbs. With a fork, beat the egg with 2 tablespoons water.

Step 2

3 Dip the filled chicken breasts first in the flour, then in the egg, then dredge in the bread crumbs. Lightly press the breading onto the chicken. Heat the oil in a deep medium skillet to 375°F.

4 Fry the chicken for about 4 minutes on each side, until golden brown. Remove from the pan and drain on paper towels.

5 Pull the parsley leaves from the stems. Cut the lemon lengthwise into thin wedges. Garnish the finished dish with parsley and lemon wedges.

Step 4

Preparation: 20 minutes
Cooking: 15 minutes
Per serving: 530 cal; 52 g pro;
27 g fat; 16 g carb.

TYPICALLY SWISS

Cooking with cheese is very popular in Switzerland. The best-known examples are Raclette—a rather pungent cheese that's melted over a fire and served with pickles and potatoes or bread—and cheese fondue.

COOKING TIP

The oil for frying the chicken fillets has to be sufficiently hot so that the breading does not soak up too much oil. Test the temperature by dipping a wooden cooking spoon in the oil. If little bubbles surface immediately, the oil is hot enough.

SERVING TIPS

A typical side dish in Switzerland is the famous rösti, a crispy, thick potato pancake.

Swiss wines are excellent, although not very well-known—try a Fendant.

CHICKEN FRICASSEE—THREE WAYS

From three European traditions come these home-style stews—hearty combinations of tender chicken and vegetables in a creamy sauce.

BASIC FRICASSEE

(SERVES 4)
- 3-pound chicken
- 1 carrot
- 1 celery rib
- 1 onion
- 1 garlic clove
- salt, white pepper
- 8 sprigs parsley
- 1 bay leaf
- 4 peppercorns
- 4 tablespoons butter
- 3 tablespoons all-purpose flour

A classic dish from which three delicious variations can be prepared in a snap.

1 Rinse the chicken in cold water; place in a large pot. Peel and chop the carrot, celery, onion, and garlic; add to chicken. Add 8 cups water, 1½ teaspoons salt, ½ teaspoon pepper, the parsley stems, bay leaf, and peppercorns. Bring to a boil; simmer 45 minutes, until done.

2 Cut the chicken into small chunks. Melt the butter in a large saucepan over medium-high heat, stir in the flour, and cook until golden. Add 3 cups of the broth and cooked vegetables and simmer for 10 minutes. Add the chicken. Chop and add the parsley leaves.

CHICKEN-MUSHROOM FRICASSEE IN WINE SAUCE

Preparation: 40 minutes Cooking: 1 hour

FRANCE

- ½ pound fresh mushrooms
- 2 shallots
- 1 tablespoon butter
- ⅓ cup dry white wine
- ¾ cup sour cream

3 While the chicken for the basic recipe cooks, clean and slice the mushrooms. Peel and mince the shallots.

4 Melt the butter in a large skillet over medium-high heat and sauté the shallots until transparent, 5 minutes. Add the mushrooms and sauté 7–10 minutes, until soft and all the liquid has evaporated.

5 Add the shallot mixture to the finished fricassee. Whisk in the wine and sour cream until blended, and gently heat through.

LEMONY CHICKEN FRICASSEE

Preparation: 40 minutes Cooking: 1 hour

ENGLAND

- ½ lemon
- 2 hard-cooked eggs
- ¼ cup heavy cream
- 1 garlic clove
- ¼ teaspoon Worcestershire sauce
- ¼ teaspoon ground ginger
- lemon slices for garnish

3 While the chicken for the basic recipe cooks, grate the peel from the lemon and squeeze out 2 teaspoons of its juice. Peel the eggs and cut lengthwise into fourths.

4 Add the lemon peel, lemon juice, cream, garlic, Worcestershire sauce, and ginger to the finished fricassee.

5 Garnish the fricassee with the hard-cooked egg wedges and the lemon slices.

CHICKEN FRICASSEE WITH ASPARAGUS

Preparation: 40 minutes Cooking: 1 hour

GERMANY

- 1 pound fresh green asparagus
- 4 ounces frozen green peas (1 cup), thawed
- ¼ cup heavy cream

3 While the chicken for the basic recipe cooks, bring 4 cups of water to a boil in a large saucepan. Cut off and discard the tough bottom portion of the asparagus. Cut each spear into 1-inch pieces.

4 Cook the asparagus in the boiling water just until tender, about 3 minutes. Drain.

5 Add the asparagus and peas to the finished fricassee and heat through, about 2 minutes. Stir in the cream and heat through, about 1 minute longer.

CHICKEN À LA PROVENÇALE

FRANCE

INGREDIENTS
(Serves 4)

- 4 skinless boneless chicken breast halves (1½ pounds total)
- 1 tablespoon herbes de Provence
- salt, black pepper
- 2 onions
- 2 garlic cloves
- 1 large tomato
- 1 eggplant (1 pound)
- 2 small zucchini
- 1 *each* green, yellow, and red bell pepper
- 4 tablespoons olive oil
- ¼ cup chopped parsley
- 2 tablespoons chopped fresh basil plus whole leaves for garnish

INGREDIENT TIP

When buying fresh garlic, look for firm, tight heads with either white or pink skins.

Fragrant herbs, juicy tomatoes, and vegetables sautéed in aromatic olive oil enliven this classic chicken dish, which might awaken a longing for France's sun-drenched South.

1 Rinse the chicken in cold water; pat dry and sprinkle with the herbes de Provence, ½ teaspoon salt, and ¼ teaspoon pepper. Peel the onions and garlic and dice. In a saucepan of boiling water, blanch the tomato for 30 seconds, peel, and cut into ½-inch dice. Wash the eggplant and zucchini and cut into 1-inch cubes. Cut the peppers in half; remove the seeds and veins, rinse, and cut into thin strips.

Step 1

2 Heat 2 tablespoons oil over medium-high heat in a large nonstick skillet. Sauté the chicken for 4 minutes on each side. Remove to a plate.

3 Add the remaining oil to the skillet and sauté the onions, garlic, eggplant, zucchini, and peppers for 2 minutes. Add the tomato, ½ teaspoon salt, and ¼ teaspoon pepper. Cook, stirring, for 6–7 minutes.

Step 1

4 Place chicken on vegetables, cover, and simmer over low heat for 15 minutes. Remove chicken and slice crosswise. Stir herbs into vegetables. Serve chicken over vegetables. Garnish with whole basil leaves.

Step 3

Preparation: 40 minutes
Cooking: 30 minutes
Per serving: 410 cal; 44 g pro; 16 g fat; 24 g carb.

TYPICALLY FRENCH

In sunny Provence, a region in Southern France, a variety of olives grow alongside this area's famous herbs. Most of the olives are pressed into olive oil (as shown at left), which is a staple ingredient in the region's cuisine.

COOKING TIPS

• You'll find it easy to skin the tomato if you score it on one end with a sharp knife before blanching.

• In Step 4, be sure to simmer over low heat or the vegetables will overcook and the tender chicken breasts will dry out.

SERVING TIPS

As an appetizer, spread black-olive paste or grated Parmesan cheese over baguettes, then toast them in the oven.

🍷 A lovely rosé from the south of France, such as a Tavel, goes well with this dish.

TUSCAN CHICKEN

ITALY

The sun-dappled, lush hills of Tuscany, a region in Northern Italy, are evoked in this succulent recipe: Juicy tomatoes, black olives, capers, and wine lend color and flavor.

INGREDIENTS
(Serves 4-6)

- 2 garlic cloves
- 1 sprig rosemary
- salt, black pepper
- 1 lemon
- 5 tablespoons olive oil
- 2½-pound chicken
- ¾ pound tomatoes
- ½ cup dry white wine
- 1 tablespoon tomato paste
- 2 fresh sage leaves
- ½ cup pitted Calamata olives
- 2 tablespoons capers
- 1 tablespoon anchovy paste

INGREDIENT TIPS

• If you're not an anchovy lover, omit the paste and add an extra pinch of salt.
• Try to find fresh sage, which has a more pleasant taste than the dried variety.

1 Peel the garlic, chop finely, and grind in a mortar with a few rosemary needles, and ½ teaspoon each salt and pepper. Grate the peel from the lemon. Mix the peel and 3 tablespoons oil into the garlic mixture. (Or mix everything in a food processor.)

2 Rinse the chicken in cold water, pat dry, and cut into 8 pieces. Spread the garlic mixture over the chicken, cover, and refrigerate for 1 hour. Blanch the tomatoes in boiling water for 30 seconds, peel, cut in half, and squeeze out a little of their juice.

3 Heat 1 tablespoon oil in a large nonstick skillet and sauté half the chicken until golden brown, 5 minutes per side. Remove to a plate. Repeat with remaining oil and chicken. Return all the chicken to the pan.

4 Squeeze the lemon juice into a bowl. Stir in the wine and tomato paste; add to the chicken with the tomatoes. Cover and simmer over medium heat for 15–20 minutes.

5 Mince the sage and remaining rosemary. Halve the olives. Add the herbs, olives, capers, and anchovy paste to the chicken. Remove from the heat. Let stand 5 minutes.

Step 1

Step 2

Step 5

Preparation: 20 minutes
Marinating: 1 hour
Cooking: 40 minutes
Per serving: 541 cal; 38 g pro; 41 g fat; 8 g carb.

TYPICALLY TUSCAN
Many Tuscan dishes are flavored with capers. The smaller the buds of this plant, which is indigenous to the Mediterranean, the more prized they are by cooks. After harvesting, capers are preserved in either salt or vinegar.

COOKING TIP

Try extending the tomato sauce with sliced zucchini and cubed eggplant, which you can add to the sauce along with the tomatoes. If you like your sauce particularly spicy, simply replace the black pepper with crushed red pepper flakes.

SERVING TIPS

Tuscan chicken goes especially well with Italian bread and a tossed green salad with an herbed vinaigrette.

Serve your chicken with style, accompanied by a red wine of the region, like a Chianti.

ℐHERRIED CHICKEN WINGS

SPAIN

Crispy on the outside, juicy and tender on the inside, these herbed and breaded chicken wings are delectable—and just right for a cozy meal with friends.

INGREDIENTS
(Serves 6-8)

- 5 pounds chicken wings
- 4 garlic cloves
- Salt
- 1 teaspoon minced fresh rosemary
- 1 tablespoon Tabasco sauce
- 1 cup dry sherry
- ¾ cup vegetable oil
- 1 cup all-purpose flour
- 2 cups bread crumbs
- ⅔ cup chopped parsley or chervil
- 4 eggs
- lemon slices

INGREDIENT TIP

Spaniards often use sherry, a fortified wine made in the Andalusia region of Southern Spain, in their cooking. If you prefer, substitute dry white wine or chicken broth.

1 Rinse the chicken in cold water and pat dry. Cut off the tips. Place the wings in a large shallow dish. Peel the garlic, sprinkle with ½ teaspoon salt, and crush to a paste. Place in a small bowl. Add the rosemary, Tabasco, sherry, and 2 tablespoons oil.

2 Brush the garlic mixture over the wings, cover, and refrigerate for at least 1 hour. Turn the wings occasionally.

3 Heat the remaining oil over medium-high heat in a large nonstick skillet. In a large plastic food-storage bag, mix the flour, 2 teaspoons salt, and ½ teaspoon pepper. In another bag, mix the bread crumbs and parsley. Whisk the eggs in a large bowl.

4 Working with one fourth of the wings at a time, drain them slightly, and place in the bag with the flour. Shake to coat. Then dip into egg to coat and place in the bag with the bread crumbs. Shake to coat.

5 Fry the pieces in oil on each side for 10–12 minutes, until golden brown, and drain on paper towels on a platter. Keep warm in a 200°F oven while you fry the remaining batches. Serve with lemon slices.

Step 1

Step 2

Step 5

Preparation: 50 minutes
Marinating: 1 hour
Cooking: 50 minutes
Per serving: 568 cal; 28 g pro;
35 g fat; 33 g carb.

TYPICALLY SPANISH
During the Middle Ages, the Moors occupied nearly all of Spain and influenced everything from architecture to cuisine. Particularly in Southern Spain, one can detect a Moorish accent to this day.

COOKING TIP

Instead of discarding the tips of the chicken wings, save them to make a superb base for broth: Boil them in 8 cups of water with your choice of spices and soup vegetables. Let this simmer for 3 hours, then use the resulting stock in a soup, or let it cook down and store the broth in ice-cube trays.

SERVING TIPS

Baked potatoes, served with sour cream or garlic mayonnaise, make a satisfying side dish.

A full-bodied Spanish red wine, such as a Rioja, rounds out the flavor of this meal.

SERVING TIPS The ideal accompaniment to this dish is a generous portion of yellow rice.

 Try a glass of dry (*fino*) sherry as an aperitif; it is best when served slightly chilled.

$\mathcal{A}$NDALUSIAN CHICKEN TARRAGON

SPAIN

INGREDIENTS
(Serves 4)

- 4 skinless boneless chicken breast halves (about 1 pound total)
- 8–10 shallots
- 1 lemon
- 2 tablespoons olive oil
- salt, black pepper
- ½ cup chicken broth
- ⅓ cup dry sherry
- ¼ cup chopped fresh tarragon
- 2 tablespoons sour cream

INGREDIENT TIP
Tarragon is an aromatic yet pungent herb. If you can't find any fresh tarragon, you can substitute one teaspoon of the dried herb.

The fresh, exquisite aroma of this dish—chicken breast halves simmered in a sauce finely seasoned with sherry and tarragon—will lure your guests to the table.

1 Wash the chicken in cold water and pat dry. Peel the shallots. Remove the yellow peel from the lemon with a vegetable peeler (avoid the bitter white pith), then cut into fine shreds and place in a small bowl. Add 1 tablespoon lemon juice and set aside.

2 Heat the oil in a large skillet over medium-high heat. Sprinkle the chicken with ½ teaspoon salt and ¼ teaspoon pepper and sauté for 4–5 minutes on each side. Transfer to a plate. Reduce the heat to medium and cook the whole shallots, stirring, for about 5 minutes, until they are soft and translucent.

3 Increase the heat to medium-high. Add the chicken broth, sherry, lemon juice, and lemon peel. Boil the sauce, scraping to deglaze.

4 Add the chicken to the sauce; cover and simmer over medium heat for 4–5 minutes. Remove the chicken and shallots. Cut the chicken into thick diagonal slices and arrange with shallots on warm plates. Whisk the tarragon, sour cream, ½ teaspoon salt, and ¼ teaspoon pepper into the sauce and serve with the chicken.

Step 2

Step 4

Step 4

Preparation: 20 minutes
Cooking: 30 minutes
Per serving: 246 cal; 27 g pro; 10 g fat; 5 g carb.

TYPICALLY ANDALUSIAN
Jerez de la Frontera is the name of a town in the Andalusian region of Southern Spain—and also the name of its famous sherry. In the sherry-making process, young wine is aged in oak casks, where it sits until the cellar master gives his final blessing.

$\mathcal{Z}$ESTY CHICKEN PIRI-PIRI

PORTUGAL

A little red chile pepper provides the heat and highlights in this vibrant dish from sunny Portugal. It's a sure-fire hit with those who love their fare on the hot side.

INGREDIENTS
(Serves 4)

- 1½ pounds skinless boneless chicken breast halves
- 1 large red bell pepper
- 1 Thai bird chile pepper or ½ teaspoon crushed red pepper
- 2 garlic cloves
- 2 tablespoons olive oil
- ½ cup dry white wine
- 1 cup Calamata olives
- salt, black pepper
- ½ bunch fresh parsley

INGREDIENT TIP

As an alternative, you can use any small red chile, such as a serrano chile, in this dish.

1 Rinse the chicken in cold water, pat dry, and cut into thin strips. Seed and devein the bell pepper and cut into thin strips. Trim and mince the chile. Peel the garlic cloves and mince.

2 Heat 1 tablespoon oil in a large skillet. Over medium-high heat, sauté the chicken for 4–5 minutes, until golden brown, stirring constantly. Transfer to a bowl, then set aside.

3 Heat the remaining oil in the skillet, add the bell pepper, chile, and garlic, and sauté for 2–3 minutes. Increase the heat to high, add the wine, and boil for 1–2 minutes, until the liquid is reduced by half. Add the chicken, olives, and ¼ teaspoon black pepper. Cover and simmer for 10 minutes over medium heat.

4 While the chicken cooks, rinse the parsley in cold water, pat dry, and finely chop the leaves. Sprinkle the chicken with the parsley and serve.

Step 1

Step 3

Step 4

Preparation: 20 minutes
Cooking: 20 minutes
Per serving: 376 cal; 40 g pro;
18 g fat; 11 g carb.

TYPICALLY PORTUGUESE
Chile peppers were introduced from South America to Portugal by conquistadores in the 16th century. The dish above is inspired by the Portuguese hot pepper sauce called piri-piri, which is used as a fiery seasoning.

COOKING TIPS

• It's a good idea to don rubber gloves before cleaning chiles, since the hot oil can cling to your hands for a long time.

• If you don't like very spicy food, cut chiles into larger pieces or cook whole—then you can remove them with a fork before serving the dish.

SERVING TIPS

Offer a hearty soup of cabbage, sausage, onions, and potatoes as a first course.

Enjoy the meal with sangria, the fruity wine punch that's as popular in Portugal as it is in Spain.

*M*EDITERRANEAN LEMON CHICKEN

GREECE

This tangy lemon chicken, gently stewed with carrots and celery in a fragrant vegetable broth, is a distinctive Mediterranean delicacy from Greece.

INGREDIENTS
(Serves 4-6)

- 3-pound chicken
- 2 lemons
- 1 onion
- 2 carrots
- 1 celery rib
- 3 tablespoons olive oil
- ½ cup vegetable or chicken broth
- salt
- pinch of cayenne pepper
- 6-8 sprigs Italian parsley
- 2 tablespoons butter

INGREDIENT TIP

Buy lemons that seem especially heavy for their size—they're the juiciest. You'll get the most juice out of a room-temperature lemon, especially if you roll it back and forth on a hard surface before squeezing.

1 Rinse the chicken in cold water, pat dry, and cut into 8 pieces with poultry scissors. With a sharp knife, cut off the yellow peel from one of the lemons (avoid any of the bitter white pith), and cut it into fine shreds. Place it in a bowl, and add the juice of both lemons. Set aside.

2 Peel and dice the onion. Peel the carrots. Cut the carrots and celery rib crosswise into thin slices, reserving some celery leaves for garnish.

3 Heat the oil in a large skillet over medium-high heat. Sauté the chicken on all sides, 12–14 minutes in all, and transfer to a bowl. Add the vegetables to the skillet and sauté for 5 minutes. Add the chicken, reserved lemon peel and juice, the broth, ½ teaspoon salt, and the cayenne pepper.

4 Cover and simmer over low heat for 30 minutes. Rinse the parsley and pull off the leaves. Chop the parsley with the celery leaves; add to the pan. Whisk the butter into the cooking juices just until melted.

Step 1

Step 2

Step 4

Preparation: 35 minutes
Cooking: 50 minutes
Per serving: 543 cal; 35 g pro; 41 g fat; 8 g carb.

TYPICALLY GREEK

Lemons grow abundantly in Greece. Under the powerful Mediterranean sun, the green fruits transform into a ripe, glowing yellow. Lemon juice is used liberally in many Greek dishes, and the peel of the fruit often adds a colorful garnish.

COOKING TIPS

• Here's the best way to chop up the chicken for this dish: First, cut off the wings, then the legs. Next, cut the bird along the back and through the middle of the breastbone. Then cut these halves into fourths.
• If you like, you can try preparing this dish with fresh basil instead of parsley.

SERVING TIPS

A fresh, round Greek bread or rice pilaf will go nicely with this dish.

Follow up your meal with a glass of iced ouzo, an anise-flavored liqueur favored by the Greeks.

$\mathcal{F}$RAGRANT CHICKEN PILAF

TURKEY

This tasty pilaf—chicken chunks, toothsome tomatoes, exotic seasonings, and rice—is cooked with care and served in its Turkish homeland on special occasions.

INGREDIENTS

(Serves 4)

- 1 pound skinless boneless chicken breasts
- 1 medium onion
- 2 garlic cloves
- ½ pound plum tomatoes
- 3 tablespoons vegetable oil
- pinch of saffron threads
- ½ cup chicken broth
- 1 dried chile
  or ½ teaspoon crushed red pepper
- 1¼ cups long-grain rice
- ½ cup raisins
- ¼ cup pine nuts
- ½ teaspoon ground cumin
- salt, black pepper
- 1 tablespoon shredded fresh parsley

INGREDIENT TIP

Pine nuts are available in most supermarkets, but if you like, use skinned slivered almonds instead.

1 Rinse the chicken in cold water, pat dry, and cut it into ½-inch cubes. Peel the onion and garlic and finely chop. In a large saucepan of boiling water, blanch the tomatoes, peel, and cut into ¼-inch dice.

2 Heat the oil in a large skillet. Sauté the onion and garlic over medium-high heat for 1 minute, stirring constantly. Add the chicken; cook, stirring, for 4 minutes. Stir the saffron into the chicken broth. Add it to the skillet; bring to a boil. Simmer for 1 minute.

3 Crush the dried chile and add to the chicken mixture. Stir in the tomatoes, 2 cups water, the rice, raisins, pine nuts, cumin, 1½ teaspoons salt, and ¼ teaspoon black pepper.

4 Cover and cook the pilaf over low heat for 25 minutes, stirring occasionally, and, if necessary, adding water as needed. Sprinkle the parsley over the pilaf. Serve warm.

Step 1

Step 3

Step 3

Preparation: 20 minutes
Cooking: 35 minutes
Per serving: 563 cal; 34 g pro; 17 g fat; 68 g carb.

TYPICALLY TURKISH

What would a sumptuous Turkish evening be without raki, that spicy anise liqueur? This potent drink made of figs and raisins is heartily enjoyed—often with a few puffs of a water pipe—during the after-dinner social rounds of an evening.

COOKING TIP

If you like, you can vary the pilaf by adding extra vegetables, which provide a delicious boost of color and fiber. While you're frying the meat in this recipe, add some cubed, unpeeled eggplant. During the last 5 minutes of cooking (Step 4), add some chopped red and green bell pepper to the pan.

SERVING TIPS

Try this with a green salad or a side dish of cucumber cubes tossed with yogurt and garlic.

On a cool night, complement this dish with a hot cup of tea garnished with a sprig of fresh mint.

Kitchen Glossary

From A to Z, our glossary explains some of the lesser-known ingredients and cooking terms that you'll find in this book.

Bamboo Shoots

These crunchy, ivory-colored sprouts are cut young, before the bamboo has formed its bark. They're sold fresh and whole or canned and sliced.

Chervil

A tender herb that's similar in appearance to parsley, chervil has a slightly peppery flavor. It should be added at the end of cooking.

Chili Sauce

Made from chile peppers, this Asian sauce ranges in heat from spicy to fiery. It's best used sparingly. American-style chili sauce is tomato-based and much milder.

Tender and Versatile Chicken

It's low in calories and delicious, and it's suitable for so many dishes—no wonder chicken is loved around the world!

Chicken or hen?

Say what you will—it means the same thing. The animal can be male or female. The birds are generally fattened for 5 or 6 weeks and usually weigh between 2 and 3 pounds.

Whole or in pieces?

Chicken is available either whole or in pieces. The breasts are particularly lean and tender and are excellent for frying. Juicier and more appropriate for stewing or grilling are the thighs, legs, and wings.

Cutting up a whole chicken

This is easiest with a sharp knife or poultry shears. First, remove the thighs from the rump. Then remove the wings at the shoulder joint along with a small piece of the breast. Split the collarbone and part the back. Then cut off both the right and left breast fillets from the breastbone.

Using frozen chicken

To defrost a frozen chicken, remove it from the packaging, place it in a colander, and place the colander, covered, in a bowl; this way, the juice can drain away while the meat is thawing. Always thaw chicken in the refrigerator; it will take at least 12 hours for a whole bird. Chicken parts will defrost more quickly. To prevent the spread of salmonella bacteria, you should throw away the liquid produced during the thaw, rinse the chicken well, and pat it dry with paper towels, then scrub all work surfaces.

Dredging

This cooking technique involves lightly coating chicken (or other meats) with flour,

cornmeal, or bread crumbs. Dredging helps to seal in moisture and adds texture.

Ginger

A versatile seasoning that, depending on the quantity, can impart a sweet, pungent flavor or a sharp spiciness. The fresh rhizome, which you can find in the vegetable section of your grocery store, offers a particularly nice bite. Look for firm, smooth, mold-free roots. Peel ginger before using it, then chop or grate.

Herbes de Provence

An aromatic dried herb mixture created with the popular accents of Southern French cuisine. It commonly includes basil, thyme, rosemary, sage, fennel seeds, lavender, bay leaves, and marjoram.

The Wok

The large deep pan often used in Asian cooking. It's particularly suitable for stir-frying.

The classic wok

Most woks have a rounded base and come with a ring stand that fits a gas burner. For an electric stove, you'll need a wok with a flat base. Also popular are electric woks, which sit on the countertop.

The proper oil

Use an oil of neutral flavor that can be heated to high temperatures, such as peanut or soybean oil.

Preparing the ingredients

All of the necessary ingredients should be prepped before you begin to cook because you'll need to add them to the wok in quick succession.

Caring for your wok

Before using a new wok, wash it, pat dry, then heat it up with a bit of oil until the oil begins to smoke. Wipe out the oil, then let cool. Finally, rub the wok all over with more oil. It's best to apply oil after each use.

Marinade

A heavily seasoned mixture—often including herbs, spices, oil, vinegar, wine, and other accents, such as fresh ginger—in which meat steeps for several hours or longer.  It can lend extraordinary flavor, and also often serves as a tenderizer.

Pilaf

This rice dish is cooked in a manner similar to Italian risotto. The rice is first sautéed in butter or oil with various other ingredients, such as vegetables and meat or fish, and is then simmered in broth.

Rice Wine

This wine has been an important staple in Chinese cuisine for over two thousand years. It has a pale amber color and a slightly sweet, nutty taste. Rice wine is easily found in Asian markets, but sherry makes a good substitute.

Saffron

Saffron is a spice derived from the stigmas of a type of purple crocus. Dried and sold either in strands or ground to a powder, saffron adds a pungent, earthy flavor and a bright yellow color wherever it's added.

Sesame Oil

Made from toasted sesame seeds, highly flavorful sesame oil is used drop by drop to season dishes after cooking. It's sold in two varieties—light and dark. The latter has a stronger fragrance and character.

Sesame Seeds

These small seeds range in color from black to off-white. When toasted, they develop a pronounced nutty flavor and scent.

Sprouts

Available year-round, fresh bean sprouts are crispy and have a subtle flavor. They should be eaten raw (sprinkled over a dish before serving) or cooked very briefly. A canned version is sold in most food markets.

Stir-Fry

A method where cut-up ingredients are cooked very quickly in oil or butter over high heat, with constant stirring.

Tortillas

Thin, round pancakes made from corn or wheat flour that are offered at almost every Mexican meal.

Turmeric

A slightly bitter, yellow-orange spice made from the ground dried root of a tropical plant in the ginger family. Turmeric is popular in Indian and Middle Eastern cuisines and is sometimes called for as a substitute for saffron, which gives food a similar yellow color.

Menu Suggestions

Surprise your guests with a deliciously exotic dinner—maybe something from their favorite vacation spot. We hope our serving suggestions for appetizers, side dishes, or desserts help you with your meal planning. Or create your own international menu ideas!

INDIA

FRUITED CHICKEN CURRY P. 6
Cucumber-Tomato Salad with Cumin
Mango Sorbet

— ◆ —

THAILAND

CRUNCHY CASHEW CHICKEN P. 8
Carrot and Bok Choy Salad
Coconut Rice
Sliced Pineapple

— ◆ —

SINGAPORE

CHICKEN-NOODLE STIR-FRY P. 10
Spring Rolls with Hot Chili Sauce
Toffee Apples

— ◆ —

JAPAN

GOLDEN CHICKEN TERIYAKI P. 12
Miso Soup with Tofu
Fruit Salad and Green Tea

— ◆ —

AUSTRALIA

HONEY-MUSTARD CHICKEN SALAD P. 16
Whole Grain Bread and Cheese
Orange Marmalade Tarts

— ◆ —

USA

COLORFUL CHICKEN 'N RICE P. 18
Black Bean Soup
Flambéed Bananas

— ◆ —

TASTY CHICKEN BURGERS P. 20
Coleslaw
Hot Fudge Sundaes

— ◆ —

TRINIDAD

CREOLE CHICKEN CON PIÑA P. 22
Curried Potato Croquettes
Fresh Papaya with Lime

— ◆ —

JAMAICA

COCONUT-FRIED CHICKEN P. 24
Rice and Peas
Pineapple Bread Pudding

— ◆ —

MEXICO

SPICY CHICKEN MEXICANA P. 26
Sliced Avocado Salad
Cinnamon Rice Pudding

— ◆ —

CHICKEN AND BEAN ENCHILADAS P. 28
Mexican Bean Salad
Almond Cookies with Hot Chocolate

— ◆ —

MOROCCO

SPICED CHICKEN TAGINE P. 30
Couscous
Melon Salad with Mint

— ◆ —

HONEY-CITRUS CHICKEN
P. 32
Chickpea Salad
Fresh Dates and Mint Tea
— ◆ —

LEBANON
FRUIT AND RICE–STUFFED CHICKEN BREASTS P. 34
Grilled Eggplant
Walnut Baklava
— ◆ —

UKRAINE
CHICKEN KIEV P. 36
Herring Salad with Beets
Strawberries and Cream
— ◆ —

HUNGARY
CREAMY CHICKEN PAPRIKASH P. 38
Garlicky Mushrooms in Sour Cream
Walnut-Stuffed Pears
— ◆ —

AUSTRIA
CRISPY-COATED CHICKEN P. 40
Butter Roasted Potatoes
Apple Strudel with Vanilla Sauce
— ◆ —

SWITZERLAND
CHICKEN GRUYÈRE P. 42
Arugula Salad
Chocolate and Cherry Torte
— ◆ —

FRANCE
CHICKEN À LA PROVENÇALE P. 46
Cream of Pumpkin Soup
Chocolate Mousse
— ◆ —

ITALY
TUSCAN CHICKEN P. 48
Bruschetti with Tomatoes
Tiramisu
— ◆ —

SPAIN
SHERRIED CHICKEN WINGS P. 50
Gazpacho
Caramel Flan
— ◆ —

ANDALUSIAN CHICKEN WITH TARRAGON P. 52
Rice Pilaf
Sliced Oranges and Butter Cookies
— ◆ —

PORTUGAL
ZESTY CHICKEN PIRI-PIRI P. 54
Spinach Soup
Almond Torte
— ◆ —

GREECE
MEDITERRANEAN LEMON CHICKEN P. 56
Tomato-Feta Salad
Yogurt with Honey and Nuts
— ◆ —

TURKEY
FRAGRANT CHICKEN PILAF P. 58
Zucchini in Tomato Sauce
Pistachio Cake
— ◆ —

RECIPE INDEX

Photo Credits
Book cover and recipe photos:
©International Masters Publishers AB; Eising Food Photography, Dorothee Gôdert, Peter Rees, Manuel Schnell.
Agency photographs:
Introduction: Look: Heeb, Page 5 upper right. Tony Stone: Allison, page 4 lower left; Atkinson, page 4 upper left; DeVore, pages 4, 5 upper middle; Everts, page 5 lower right; Huber, pages 4, 5 lower middle.
Photos for the 'Typically' sections: Anthony Blake: page 46.
Cephas: Blythe, page 12; Kielty, page 41; Rock, page 53.
Comstock: pages 8, 20.
Garden Picture Library: Viard, page 54; Lamontagne, page 48.
Robert Harding: pages 23, 24; Frerck, pages 28, 32.
Hutchison: Egan, page 36.
The Image Bank: Eriksson, page 18.
Impact: Cormack, page 38; Edwards, page 6; Fear, page 16.
Harry Smith Collection: page 11.
Tony Stone: page 42; Armand, page 24; Hiser, page 26; Sitton, page 50; Tweedie, page 31.
Telegraph Colour Library: Moss, page 58; The Stock Directory, page 56.